THIS BOOK BELONGS TO

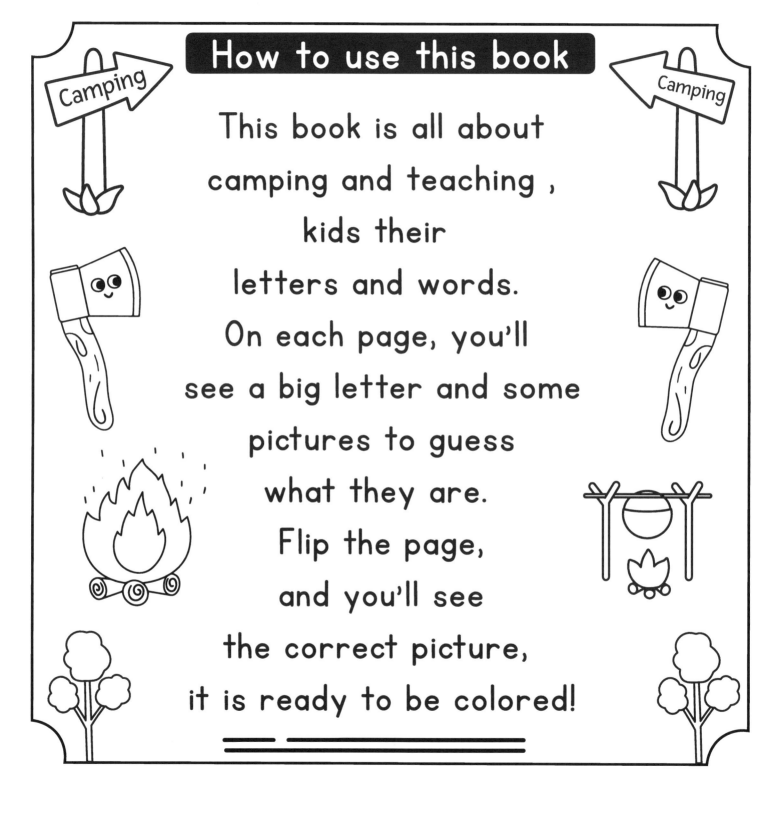

How to use this book

This book is all about
camping and teaching ,
kids their
letters and words.
On each page, you'll
see a big letter and some
pictures to guess
what they are.
Flip the page,
and you'll see
the correct picture,
it is ready to be colored!

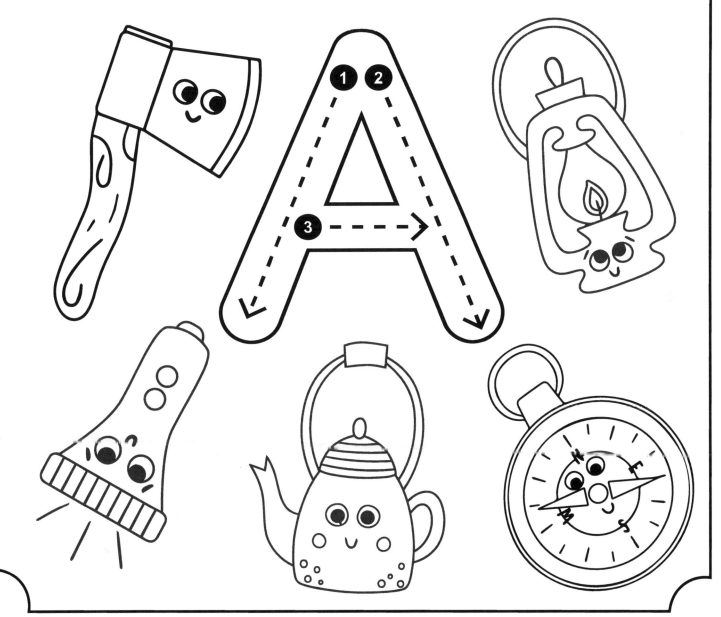

A Is for

Axe

With my little eye, i can see an object Starting with the letter...

B Is for

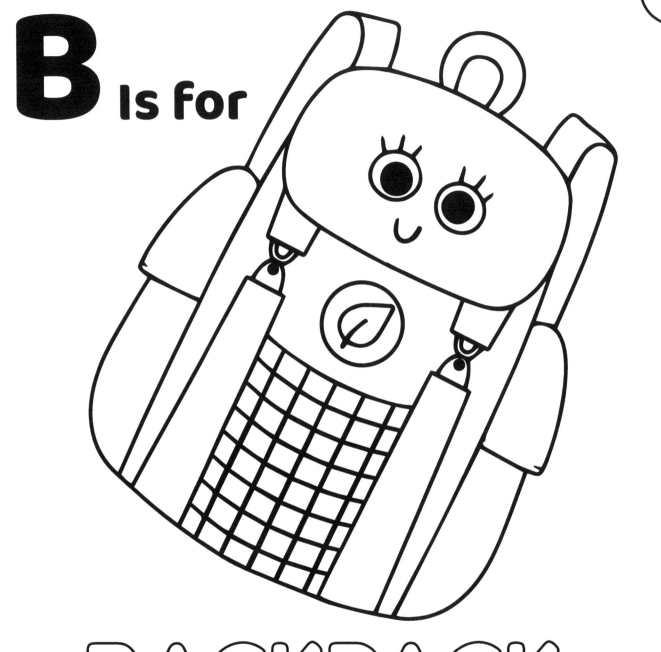

BACKPACK

With my little eye, i can see an object Starting with the letter...

C Is for

CAMP FIRE

With my little eye, i can see an object Starting with the letter...

D Is for

DECK CHAIR

With my little eye, i can see an object Starting with the letter...

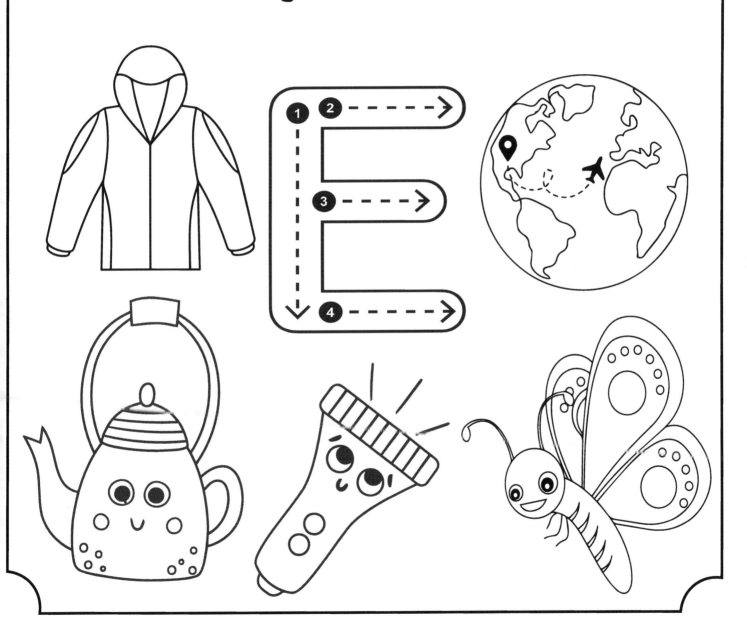

E Is for

EARTH GLOBE

With my little eye, i can see an object Starting with the letter...

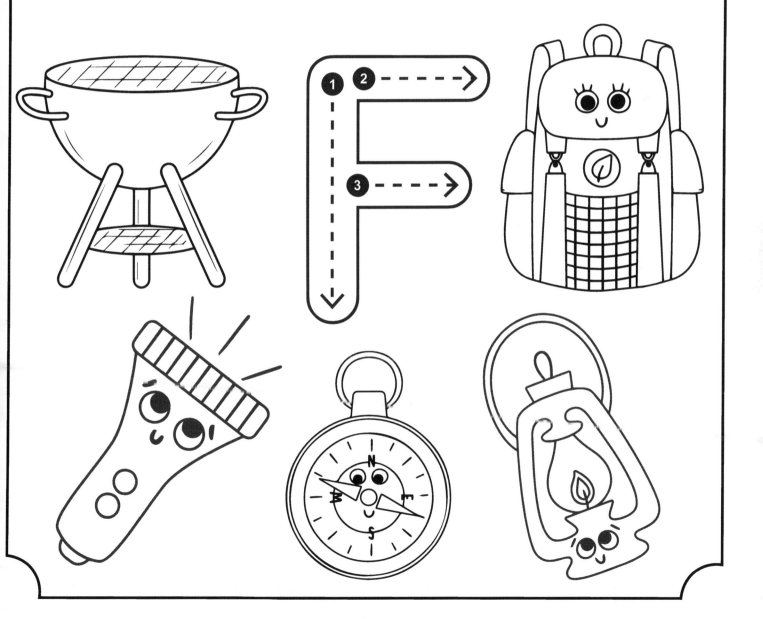

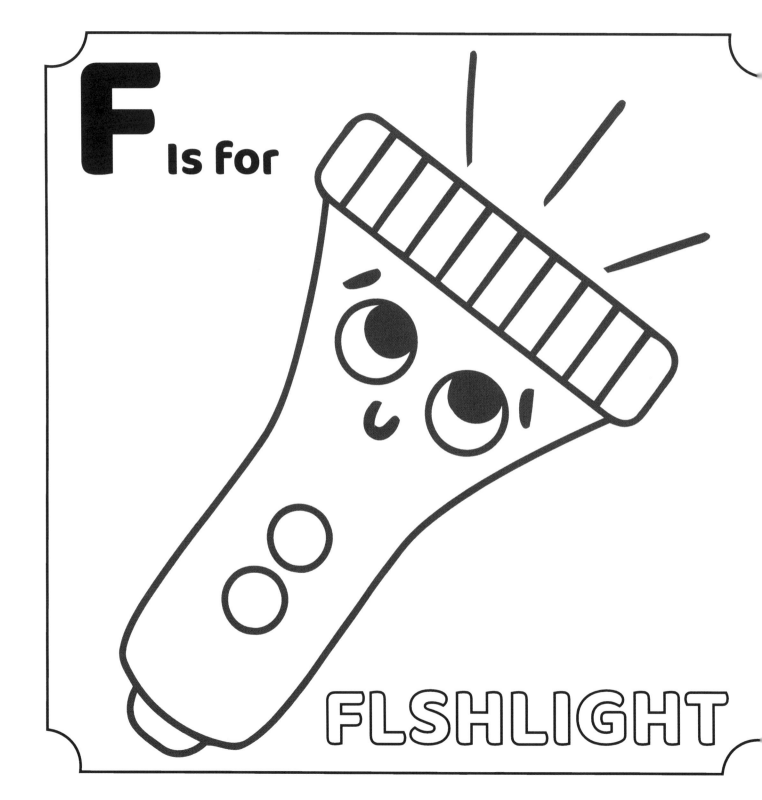

F Is for

FLSHLIGHT

With my little eye, i can see an object Starting with the letter...

With my little eye, i can see an object
Starting with the letter...

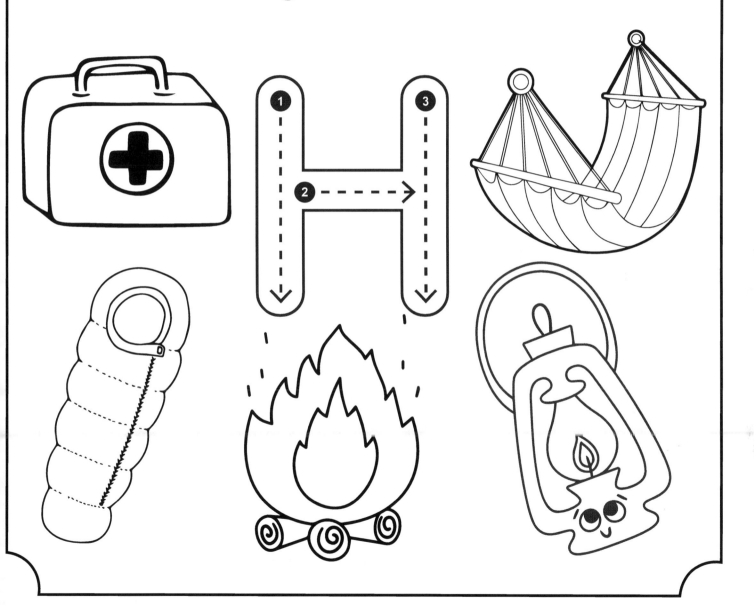

H Is for

HAMMOCK

With my little eye, i can see an object Starting with the letter...

I Is for

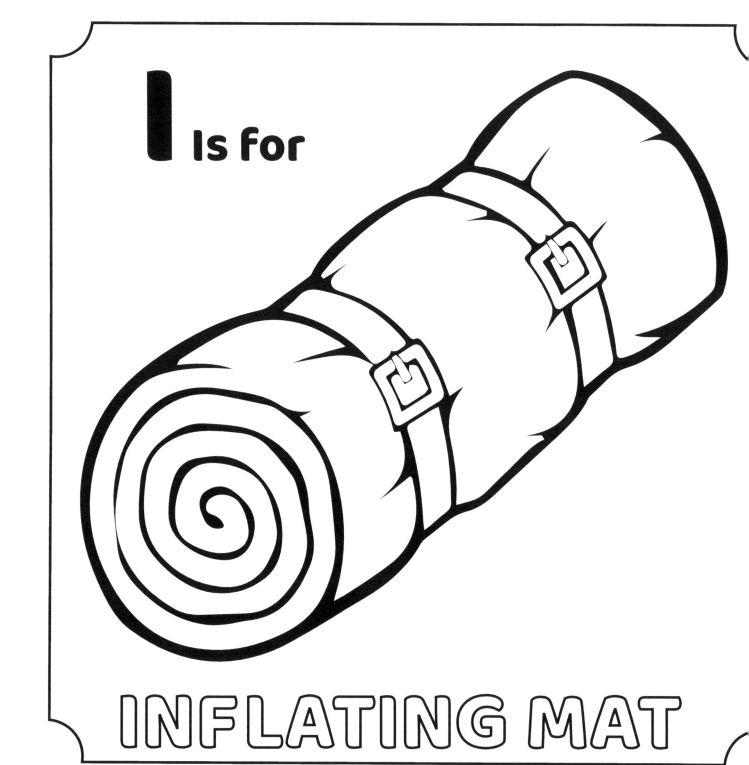

INFLATING MAT

With my little eye, i can see an object Starting with the letter...

With my little eye, i can see an object Starting with the letter...

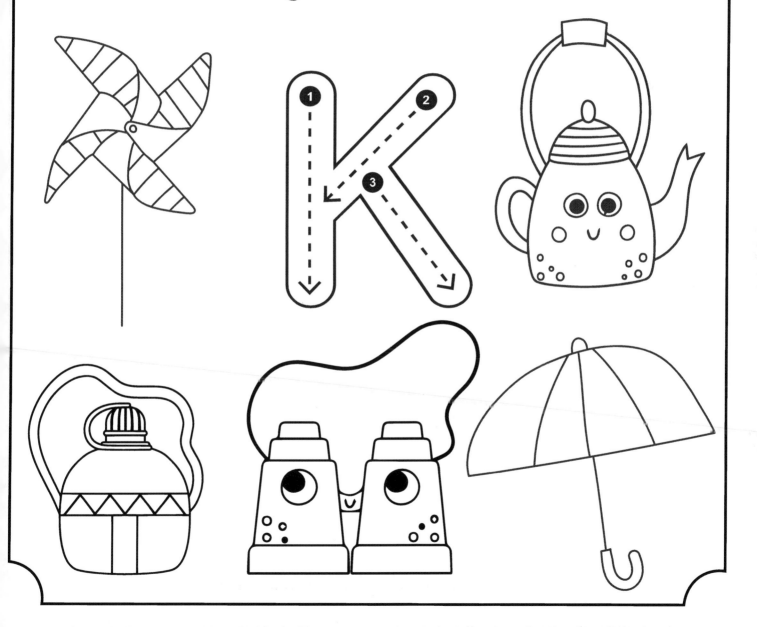

K Is for

KETTLE

With my little eye, i can see an object
Starting with the letter...

L Is for

LANTERN

With my little eye, i can see an object Starting with the letter...

M Is for
MUG

With my little eye, i can see an object Starting with the letter...

N Is for

NET

With my little eye, i can see an object Starting with the letter...

With my little eye, i can see an object Starting with the letter...

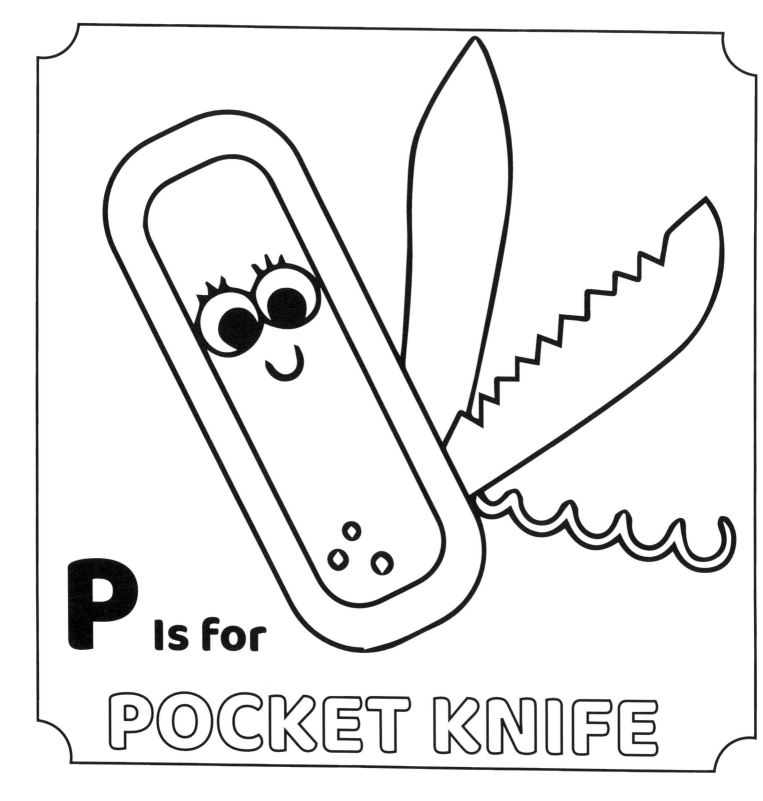

P Is for

POCKET KNIFE

With my little eye, i can see an object Starting with the letter...

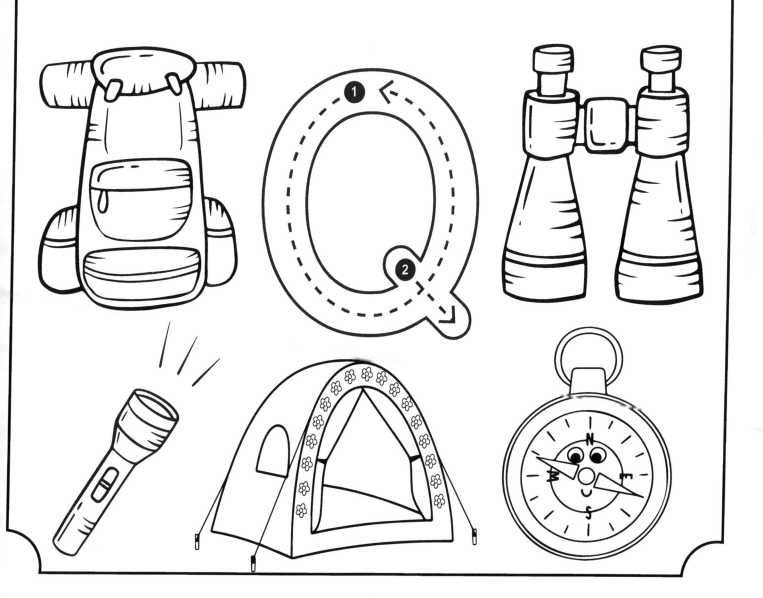

With my little eye, i can see an object
Starting with the letter...

With my little eye, i can see an object Starting with the letter...

S Is for

SLEEPING BAG

With my little eye, i can see an object Starting with the letter...

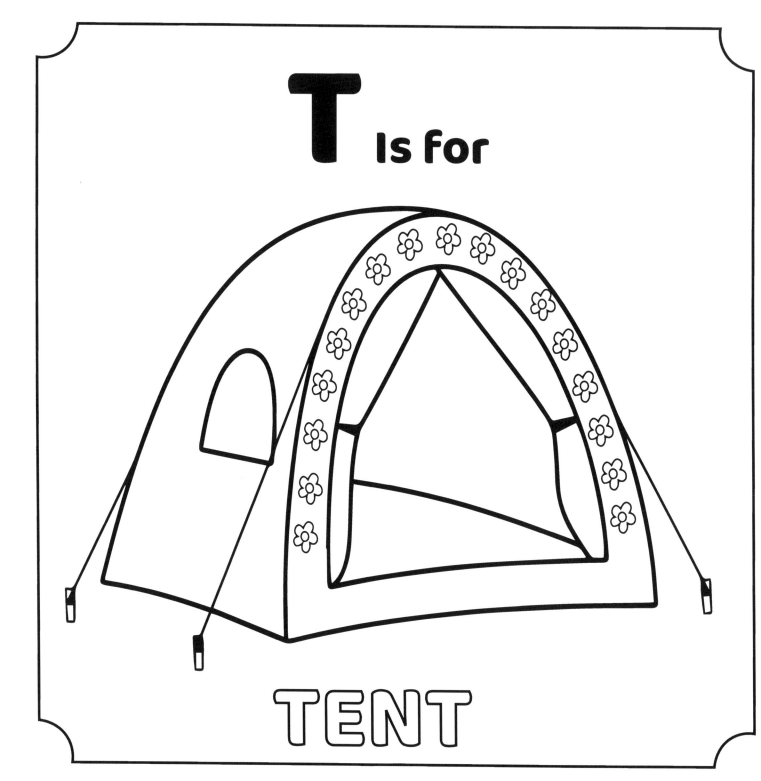

With my little eye, i can see an object Starting with the letter...

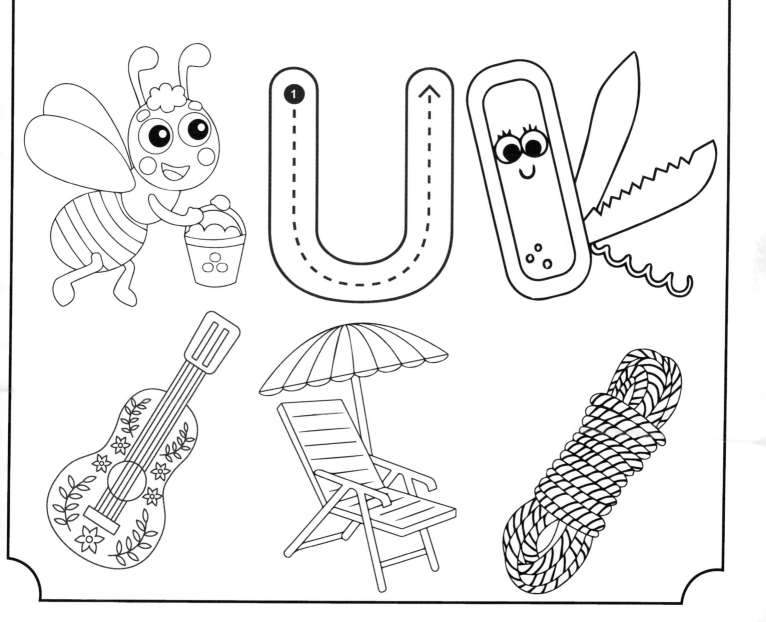

U Is for

UKULELE

With my little eye, i can see an object Starting with the letter...

V Is for

Van

With my little eye, i can see an object
Starting with the letter...

 **W** Is for

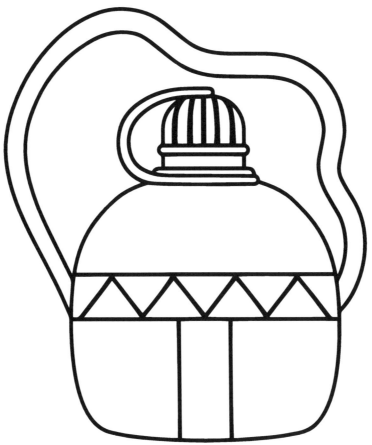

WATER BOTTLE

With my little eye, i can see an object Starting with the letter...

X Is for

XYLOPHONE

With my little eye, i can see an object Starting with the letter...

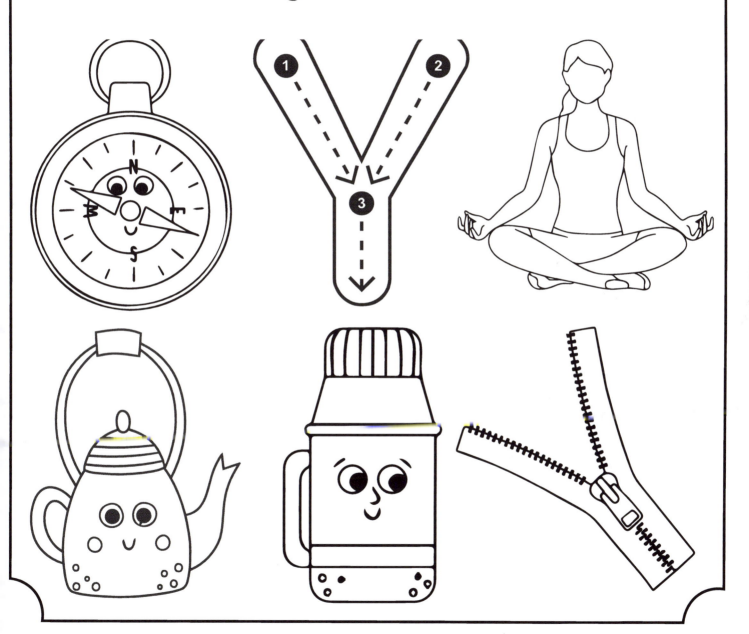

Y Is for

YOGA

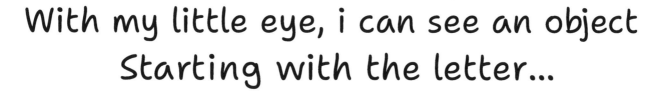

With my little eye, i can see an object Starting with the letter...

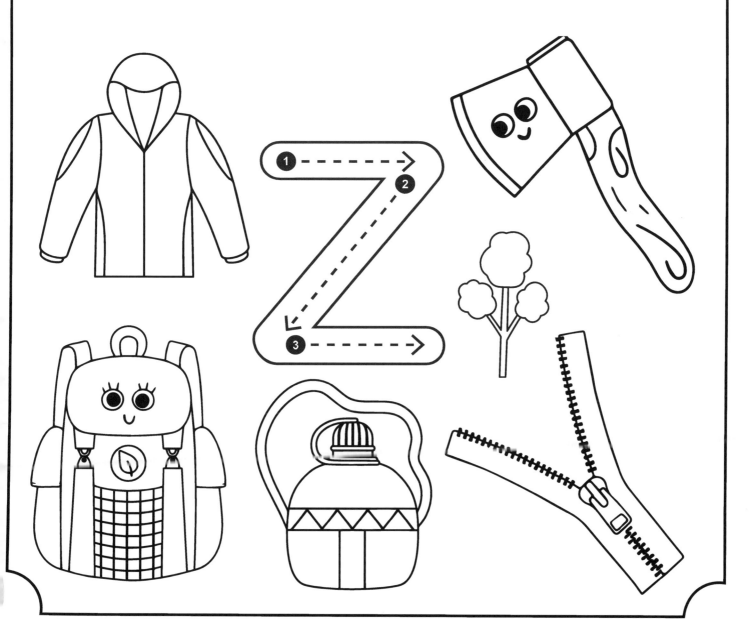

Z Is for

ZIPPER

21015017R00031